# WOMEN BONES

*poems by*

# Lauren M. Davis

*Finishing Line Press*
Georgetown, Kentucky

# WOMEN BONES

Copyright © 2023 by Lauren M. Davis
ISBN 979-8-88838-089-5 First Edition
All rights reserved under International and Pan-American Copyright Conventions. No part of this book may be reproduced in any manner whatsoever without written permission from the publisher, except in the case of brief quotations embodied in critical articles and reviews.

## ACKNOWLEDGMENTS

"Dry Tree," "Sleeping Through the Earthquake," and "Watching Them Swim." *Apofenie Magazine, Vol. 11: The Divine* (in print) 2021.

"Inside of Women" and "The Secret." *2River Press*: Spring 2017 Issue 21.3 (in print and online).

"Martin's Guilt." *The Matador Review*: Spring 2017 (in print and online).

"The Flowers You Brought Back from Italy." *Wrath Bearing Tree*: Spring 2021 (online).

Publisher: Leah Huete de Maines
Editor: Christen Kincaid
Cover Art: Lauren M. Davis
Author Photo: Samuel Phenicie
Cover Design: Elizabeth Maines McCleavy

Order online: www.finishinglinepress.com
also available on amazon.com

Author inquiries and mail orders:
Finishing Line Press
PO Box 1626
Georgetown, Kentucky 40324
USA

# Table of Contents

Dry Tree ............................................................................. 1

The Secret ......................................................................... 4

Drawing the Body ............................................................ 6

Inside of Women .............................................................. 9

Sleeping Through the Earthquake ................................ 10

Martin's Guilt ................................................................. 12

The Flowers You Brought Back from Italy ................. 13

Storms ............................................................................. 16

Pronunciation ................................................................. 17

Watching Them Swim ................................................... 23

In the Bath ...................................................................... 25

If You Want to Be Thin ................................................. 27

## DRY TREE

Today the wind came
and knocked all the dead
     and weak
                    trees
down.

On the way out to the country,
roads are blocked,
fire and ambulance men
work to remove the fallen—
little yellow sleeves, cuffs, hardhats,
and hems speckled inside a conglomeration   of branches.

You used to cry;
everything that made you human
disoriented/
You were once that down tree,
stretched across the road,
and the one at the edge
of the riverbank, begging the wind
to roll        and fold you in.

Vertebrae bruised by rock,
chest-rib bones
so prominent under skin
that your chest would vibrate with fear
at the surface, nothing to protect
what was underneath        fluttering, brittle/

You were once named *Willowy*
by that Chinese medicine doctor:
*You, all full of wind and swaying,*
*hanging down and cracking,*
*limbs cracking        arid,*
     *body-dry,*
*mind-dry,*

and the policemen did come, and the firemen did come,
to pick you up, to lift you,
at your strident shoulder blades and rear:          a stiff plank.
You were a place
where
no verve was evident, no healthy borers,
no robin songs, no nesting squirrels.

You awoke in that hospital bed,          eyes blinking,
to someone who stood there then,
but, months later, would not stand still—
a visitor to your life.

People don't always stand
where they once          said
they always would,          trees fall,
               down,
souls fall,
people say they meant that     then
but now don't mean anything at all.

What makes us happy—is it purpose?
Is it our wild brains, healthy? Is it fostering ourselves?
Is it acceptance? Is it letting go what was before
and knowing that now,          we can fight firmer?
Is it knowing we will and can actually make it
through this life alone,
that dying alone is nothing but the safety of being human?

All debris collects
somewhere: something,
after some time, a tiny, new light,
a spruce, a seed, a morsel,
as we know,
               but so often          don't believe.

When my brain was broken, I read it could never repair.

Yet, here it is again,
full of tiny, healthy sparks,
full of making, full of water flowing,
a river which could never
dry out,                nor collapse.
You, self, will never dry out
nor collapse            again.
No.
                      *A river runs through you.*

# THE SECRET

When I forget to say *amen*
at the end of a prayer
it's like leaving something
that should be closed,
open.

Like I'm not home
and have left a window open,
and a storm has begun.

Like the rain will enter me,
flush out the things
I'm not ready to part with.

I rushed home
during that storm,
and pushed the heavy glass

up to close where I had once opened,

the water rushed like a tide,
down my forearms,
filled the empty cups of my bra
where lately            space has collected.

Papers on my desk below
absorbed the rain,
rusty water filled my mouth.

With a towel I soaked it up,
like I didn't want anybody to know:
committing to a secret.

These papers will dry
this window I can keep closed    /     shut
but my aching body
is the one
who will never forgive me,
and will never let me forget
the secret only God knows.

*Amen*, I am forgiven,
*Amen*, I must forgive myself.

## DRAWING THE BODY

there is a nude woman:
robe off,
her breast a humble offering
pointing
toward my eyes,

my head
is up against the wall,
charcoal is poised in my right hand,
its black mark is on my lips
from where I touched
them in thought,
I knead
a grey eraser gob
between
my left thumb and finger

much unnatural pull comes
from gazing upon nudity,
some kind
of shame in it,
but the artist must,
to copy flesh
onto the page,
to learn
how to drag the pencil,
smudge the charcoal,
dust the jawline, the hipbone

this nude woman is of my kind,
her full body
reminds me
of when my bones
were not exposed
when my elbows were round,
my calves strong

if I were naked here
some might shiver
at my exposed, white
notch spine,
my vulnerable
hips poking
through skin
like canvas-tents

I recently undressed my body
in a room full of women
to try on a shirt, a gift,

I turned my back
to the bridal party,
bent over to dip my head
into the opening
for the neck

and heard gasps

and when I turned around
the shirt hung and draped,
the arm holes gaped
with emptiness,

the woman took her gift back.

Now, here in front of me
is ripeness
and my breath is deep
in its presence

my eye
traces the curve of her
egg-smooth shoulders,
like a light piercing
a windowpane

I mark
the maternal shape
of her dough breasts,
deepen her supple
dimpled knees
with the dark material,

between the shaved wood
of my pencil
I find the outside
of her leg,
connect it to her belly,
draw the x in her button,

the timer chimes
when I haven't yet made it
to her face—

she pulls the robe
over her back,
ties the cotton belt
in front,
walks over
to see
what I have drawn.

## INSIDE OF WOMEN

I.

I knew a woman
who
after she swam in the ocean
was filled with its sand
and when the doctor removed it

he found inside her a pearl.

II.

Inside tiny apples my lips often find
the core absent of seeds—
many hollow stars
have reminded
that inside me a mouth
would find the same hollow,
my young body / bones too thin,
on a hunger strike.

But tiny sterile apples seem safe for eating.

## SLEEPING THROUGH THE EARTHQUAKE

Falling asleep
anywhere I could—
floors of basements,
clothes piles in closets
couches near gun shots,
tents in wildernesses,
cars abandoned,
attics, RVs, or barn lofts of friends—
I'd long for the slumber
and wake of home,
the nest it was before

I wanted to fall from it.

The faraway hum
of the train and coyote howl,
the pieces of hay
brought in by
the open window's palm
to rest on my cheek,
the soft-air close of the backdoor,
my father leaving for work,
the neigh of horses
and the swish of their white tails,
my mother singing
*Sweet Baby James*
over vacuuming.

One morning
I woke up
on a friend's porch,
wrists through the spindles,
to my telephone ringing,
a voice which was my mother
asking why
I hadn't answered throughout the night.

She said she'd been pacing
hours barefoot
on the farmhouse floors,
calling to warn me
about the earthquake.

Before it hit
she'd had a nightmare
that a crack split the earth open,
making a canyon
that forever separated
mothers from their young.

In the dream
I had fallen
off the bed of the ground,
rolled into the mouth
and turned there     into a woman.

## MARTIN'S GUILT

With your boots at my bedside,
a western window open,
I wondered where you went,
barefoot, in a place like this.

Then my eyes absorbed your face
forming in the dark air,
your hand pulling me out of bed by my sleeve
to show me the ring around the moon.

Sitting on the front porch I said:
I know              it is a long way to home.

It was a long way to where      you could trust
that you would never drive drunk,
and paralyze someone
from the neck down,         again.

Missing another night
I found you
flaying the skins of your memories,
vomiting       into the kitchen sink.

When I reached to release the faucet
you cupped the running water
like you were lifting a baby bird

and said you dreamt
that the snow came through
the western window, collected and formed
the shape of my body on the bedroom floor.

## THE FLOWERS YOU BROUGHT BACK FROM ITALY

Each time I open my notebook the pages stick.
Because I've forgotten.

And onto the ground
they fall:
royal purple flowers fall
out,
emerald stemmed, blue veined,
life
from the coast of Italy.

You pulled them from the earth,
pinched their feet
with your fingertips,

you breathed into the sea

and thought of the way my hair
swayed between my shoulders,
while you once walked behind me
near an American riverside,
flowers sway in the field
the same way.

You placed the poppies then
into the spine of your bible
you pressed it,
punched the face
and rubbed the back
onto the ground
to release water
into sacred words
you pressed,
wanting me there
and you breathed into the sea.

Yesterday, you stood in the kitchen
of your new house
while the songbirds in the yard
called good morning,
you opened your bible
and pulled the flowers up
by the end of their stems
like tails,
their faces
tumbling downward

and I opened myself / my notebook
and tossed the flowers into
my spine / my book's spine

and there
I closed it
and pressed it into the granite
underneath
to press
wanting to stay there with you
out.

You asked me:
when again do you leave?
Two weeks.

Now,
one-thousand miles away
the pages stick
each time I open my notebook

and onto the ground they fall,

and I remember how
you must have looked
collecting purple poppies
by the sea of Italy.

Our modern lives,
so set apart,
both
by miles
and unsteadiness.

**STORMS**

Sometimes we watch it pass.
Other times it floods us.

Sometimes we hear about it.
Other times it won't end.

Some of us never see it
and wonder why we are so blessed.

Sometimes we wake up to it—
we didn't know it was on its way.

Some are predictable.
Some are a consequence.

Sometimes we need it—
to nurture what we plant.

At times, we've begged or danced for it;
we've hopped and embraced it,

while it has happened
or after what we see it has left
on the ground.

## PRONUNCIATION
*on a writer's residency in Shelton, Washington*

I.

A woman named Carolyn
I just met today
takes me to her home
atop a hillside
across from a tiny library,
the kind where the homeless wait
near the front door
at opening hour
and a policeman lets them in,
one at a time.

Carolyn has brought me over
to pick arugula and raspberries.
She pronounces it *ah-roo-gew-lah*,
and has already given me
strawberries,
and two morel mushrooms
that crumple like dark paper.

Her house
is a light blue and oak
fairy tale,
her dog a sheltie,
like *Shelton*,
which I have been pronouncing Sheldon
until I heard the townspeople say it.
The foyer or foy-yay,
is thick with the smell of granola.
Raisins, oats, and blanched almonds
baking gently,
following us to the courtyard

where I peak into her husband's
tiny workshop
as Carolyn begins to pick.
A *theologian*,
she tells me
as her fingers pull
each ruby nipple
like a prayer.

I try to be
just as delicate.
But each time
I pluck
a waxy inside
is left behind.
I wonder
if I should remove it
but I don't interrupt
Carolyn's rhythmic harvest.

Yet she speaks
without breaking it.
She says
*don't put any
with the slightest mold
in the basket.
It'll ruin the whole bunch.*

We laugh with sour faces
recalling our molars
biting into
foul cherry tomatoes,
or our tongues
absorbing the black
parts of avocados,
not in able occasions to spit.

I tell her how I worked
for a strict
Midwestern country club
who fired a newly-pregnant,
uneducated salad girl
after she *sent-out*
moldy raspberries
resting inside leaves of kale,
how I found her teardrops
like a trail of blood
leading to the locker room.
Carolyn picks *arugula*
carrying the basket
underneath her breast
with the triangle of her arm.
I only watch, complementing
her Calla Lilies.

We get locked out
at the back door.
I think, maybe
I wasn't suppose
to shut it.
At the front,
near a pear tree,
she turns a tiny brass knob
with her one free hand,
and it opens.

II.

I walk alone
in a Salt Marsh in Belfair,
binoculars swinging
around
my boney neck.

I recall the names of birds
in my mind,
some of the same kind
from home:
*Red Winged Blackbird,
Common Barn Swallow,*
all in my father's voice.

Others I can place
in their major class,
but I am too far from home
to be precise,
*Warbler.*
On the way back
to my cabin in Shelton,
I stop at the library.

Before going in
I eat in the sun.
A salad of strawberries,
raspberries, *arugula*,
lemon juice, and cinnamon.

Closing my eyes
under the influence
of the salad's warm tang
my mind recites:
*one bad raspberry
ruins the whole bunch.*

The policeman watches me
twisting the fork
in my mouth,
twisting my hair
away from my neck,
pulling the fork out,
lips pressing
on its hard edges,
placing it down,
twisting my hair,
placing the band.

When I look over
he turns his head
in a flash,
straightens
his short back
and walks inside.


III.

By telephone
I tell my fiancé
I'm back
to Shelton
from driving around
the *Pungent Sound,*
he corrects me,
*Puget Sound.*

I wonder            how I'd speak
if I only ever
heard
my own words.

I tell him about
Carolyn and the salad,
I forget how
I say
*arugula.*

When I enter the library,
and the policeman
holds the door,
I say *thank you,*
giving
the pronunciation
a second thought.

## WATCHING THEM SWIM
*in the voice of a friend*

I sit on the speedboat
with a beer bottle resting on my knee,
as friends strip off their clothes,
and one by one jump
into the interrupted lake,
laughing
with the delight of liberty.

As the girls swim,
long hair twists
in the clear liquid,
weeds catch the strands,
heads bob:

A prayer that dips
atop then under the water,
each time farther away,
each time breathing out
at the surface
with the sound of spewing.

One of my buddies turns on his back,
his round face mirroring the sun,
legs pumping
somewhere underneath
like an otter tail.

Their chests fill with oxygen
and their bodies float
at the surface of the water.
They look like my bedridden mother:

Her frail arms that rested above linens
when I made the bed around her
as if she wasn't even there.

When I said I was leaving town
for a few days
she said I should be ashamed
for leaving her.
Sometimes I'm afraid
to look at her face.

At nightfall
we return to land to set up our tents
while the couple in the lot next to us
fights in a language I don't recognize.

Their son comes over
to visit us. I ask him
what the best part of his day was.

He asks me to answer first.
I tell him it was the hours
I spent watching my friends swim.

He says he played in the woods
and that his mother watched,
smiling as he climbed a rock
that was a ladder to the sun.

## IN THE BATH

Underwater
is the only place
where silence            could exist.

Water is where
our weight leaves us.

Within it we remember
we are not just a body,
but have a spirit

and the rhythm of birth
which is much like
the tasks of our days:

the push and then rest,
the push and then rest,                    the waiting,
is absent

because water holds us   nodding
in a space where we calmly
accept our solitude.

Water fills the empty visions
of our dreams,
flushes us from the boy
who while we were unwilling    filled us with his dirt.

When the drain is drawn,
water lowers us slowly,
exposes our bodies,
naked            as they were before.

When the water is gone
we feel the ache of the world again.

Somebody told me
that every seven years
our bodies are made fresh
because every cell inside of us
has died and has been replaced.

Somebody told me
all the water on earth
has been the same water        since the beginning.

## IF YOU WANT TO BE THIN

If you want to be thin,
since so many of you have asked me,
here's what to do:

spend most of your time      asleep,
laying down,
playing dead
because moving around
will make your body hungry.

Only eat a couple cups
of food at a time
three times a day,
count, carefully, 600 calories per day,
never, ever, go beyond that,
it's even better to eat below the line.

Eat no fat.
Eat no refined sugar.
You'll start to see your skeleton pretty soon.
Hungry? No you're not.
Drink water.
Chew gum.

First, when you stand side-ways
in the mirror
and place your hand on your hip,
you'll start to see the caps of your shoulders,

Then the ridges of your spine
when you bend over naked
and peer back, again at the mirror.

Next, each rib underneath
your breasts will show themselves.
Again, at the mirror,

when you lift your arms up and down
like a fat swan trying to take flight,
the skin of your non-existent breasts
will rise and fall over those ribs,
a spoiled cloth being rubbed over a washboard.

Then, when much time has passed
you'll black out at work
and people will begin to tell you
they are worried about you
instead of that you look good.
And they'll tell you what to eat:
avocado, nut butters, proteins.
Like it's that easy to cure yourself,
like you'd actually put that in your mouth
and let it store itself in all those places
you worked so hard to empty.

This is also when
you'll ask your landlord
to please turn on the heat
because it's nearly mid-winter.
Her reply will be:
*it was on when you asked the last time
and has been set at 74 since!*
So you'll stand on the heating duct
on the floor
but you won't feel anything
in the soles of your feet.
So you'll lift them up
to look at them,
like that will help,

and you'll notice
they're a beautiful

bright orange:
carrots are a helpful,
low-calorie thing to eat.

This is also when
your eyes won't have the energy
to absorb details
in a room,
differences in much of anything—
your eyes will only work well enough
to allow you to see
what is stored in memory—
when you won't be able to hear
as well either,
you'll have to ask people
what it was they said,
you'll hate loud noises
because your body
won't be able to handle it,
you'll want to be alone
because, apparently,
*depriving yourself*
*makes you go into ancient*
*primal tendencies for survival.*
This is when you'll actually
have the strong urge to growl,
even bark. You'll feel rage.

You won't menstruate
for over six years.
So you'll visit your doctor
like something else other than eating
will cure you
and she'll tell you
your height
has shrunk an inch.

You'll eat a good meal then,
just one.
You'll feel guilty about it
for days.
But after you eat it,
you'll suddenly notice objects in rooms
that you've been visiting
for months:
a clay figurine on the top of a friend's toilet,
slots for bibles on the back of your church's pews,
you'll notice a good friend's hair
has grown almost four inches,
like she pushed a button
and it all the sudden
came tumbling out of her head.

This is when you'll have to call your mother
on your way home
because you think you might faint
in your car,
trying to get to your apartment
to eat only, even under the line,
of one of your 200 calorie-per-day
miniature meals,

when boisterous men
will ask your fiancé:
*Are you feeding her?*
They'll both laugh.
Then, later that night,
your fiancé will wear
a disgusted look on his face
and pull his hand from your back
saying, *Ugh, your back...*

This is when
even the backside of your hips
will become only bone,
when you'll see the clear,
circle-triangle outline shape
that you've been suffering
so deeply for,
so strictly for,
like the red roots of a tree
digging through hard clay
for thousands of years.

Now you've done it.
Now even the high-art
fashion clothes
are too big for you
and it's almost frustrating.

Now you'll wake up to someone
shoving food into your mouth,
you'll be scratching at the IV
in your arm,
you'll get wheeled into a room
for x-rays
that you're too weak
to sit up for,
and your fiancé will stand over you,
cry next to you,
and you'll love him so deeply there,
deeper than those red roots
you've suffered for,
for thousands of years,
but even he is beginning
to not be able
to love you anymore.

So, you'll go on vacation
with your family
to Prince Edward Island,
but you'll be too weak
to walk the beach with them.
Instead, you'll play dead
on the sand,
in the sand,
you'll be the sand,
you are only sand.

And you'll watch them
walking east
collecting
shells, rocks, coral,
like you have,
usually all four of you     together,
since your childhood.
And you'll want to cry
for childhood.

They'll get smaller
like people do
when they leave you behind
because they have to.
Then smaller.

The sky over them
is getting redder, then purple,
and you want to cry there,

but your body
just can't.

Lauren M. Davis was born in New Jersey in 1988. She first studied creative writing on a National Student Exchange to the University of North Carolina-Wilmington. She obtained her Bachelor of Arts in Writing at Indiana University-Fort Wayne and a Master of Fine Arts in Creative Writing (Poetry) from the University of Southern Maine. She designed and taught *Poetry Through Literacy*, a curriculum of poetry for illiterate adults and has worked as an adjunct professor of English and humanities at the University of Saint Francis, Indiana Institute of Technology, and Ivy Tech Community College. She was the writer in residence of Hypatia in the Woods in Shelton, Washington, the keynote speaker for the NEI Poet's Society, and has taught multiple community writing workshops. Her work has appeared in several literary magazines, journals, and an anthology. She currently lives in Indiana with her husband, their newborn daughter, and their beloved dog.

www.ingramcontent.com/pod-product-compliance
Lightning Source LLC
Chambersburg PA
CBHW022126090426
42743CB00008B/1019